For Celia Daisy
M. J.

For Gary, Mary, Mark,
and Catherine — the James Gang
D. P.

Text copyright © 1996 by Martin Jenkins
Illustrations copyright © 1996 by David Parkins

First U.S. edition 1996

Library of Congress Cataloging-in-Publication Data is available.
Library of Congress Catalog Card Number 96-2073

ISBN 1-56402-896-8

2 4 6 8 10 9 7 5 3 1

Printed in Hong Kong

This book was typeset in Weiss.
The pictures were done in ink line
and watercolor.

Candlewick Press
2067 Massachusetts Avenue
Cambridge, Massachusetts 02140

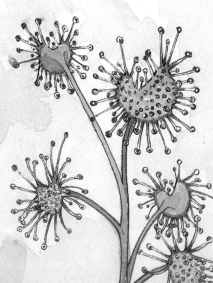

Fly Traps!

Plants That Bite Back

Martin Jenkins

illustrated by

David Parkins

CANDLEWICK PRESS
CAMBRIDGE, MASSACHUSETTS

People do all sorts of things in their spare time.

There are people who collect yogurt containers and people who make models out of bottle tops.

There are beetle hunters and giant-leek growers.

Me, I like watching plants
that eat animals.

Plants that eat animals are called
carnivorous plants.

There are hundreds of different kinds
and they grow all around the world.

It all started with a plant I found in a pond. It had little yellow flowers sticking out of the water. Under the water there were tangled stems with hundreds of tiny bubbles on them. A friend told me it was called a bladderwort.

There are over
200 different kinds of
bladderworts. Most of them
grow in ponds and rivers.
They are usually very
small, with narrow
leaves and stems.

9

She said the bubbles on the stems were the bladders. Each one had a trap door shut tight, with little trigger hairs around it.

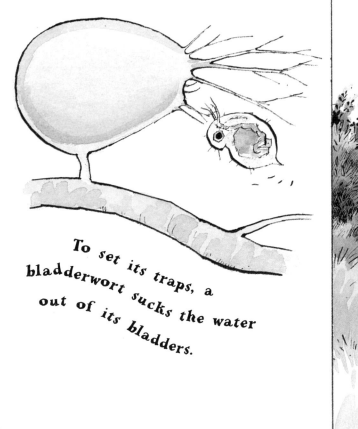

To set its traps, a bladderwort sucks the water out of its bladders.

Whenever a water flea or other bug touched a hair, the trap door swung back and in the bug went.

When a trap door opens, water rushes in, dragging the bug in with it.

Then the trap door slammed shut and there was no way out. And it all happened in the blink of an eye.

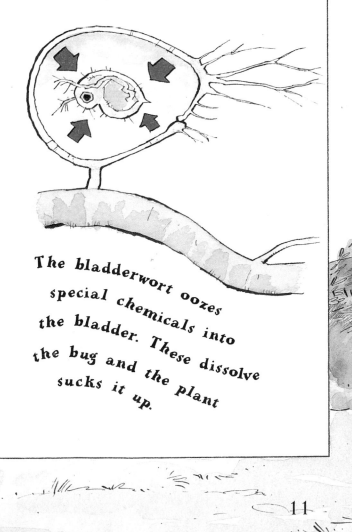

The bladderwort oozes special chemicals into the bladder. These dissolve the bug and the plant sucks it up.

Wow, that's neat, I thought. The trouble was, the traps on my plant were so small and so quick that I couldn't really see them work.

Well, I decided, I'll just have to find a bigger carnivorous plant. So I did.

I had to climb a mountain, mind you, and walk through all its boggiest, mossiest places.

But there in the moss were little red plants, shining in the sun. I thought they were covered in dewdrops, but they weren't. They were sundews, and the shiny parts were sticky like honey. I'm sure you can guess what they were for.

When a bug gets stuck on a sundew, the leaf slowly curls up around it.

Then the soft parts of the bug are dissolved by chemicals and eaten.

12

I had to leave the sundews when the clouds rolled in. But as soon as I got home, I sent away for some sundew seeds of my own.

Afterward, the leaf opens up again and the leftover bug parts fall off.

Butterworts are carnivorous plants, too, and often grow in the same places as sundews. They have flat leaves like flypaper. Little bugs stick to the leaves and slowly dissolve.

13

The seeds weren't just for ordinary sundews, though. They were for Giant African sundews. I sowed them in a pot of moss and covered it with glass.

I watered the pot every day with rainwater straight from the water tank. Soon the seeds started to sprout and I had dozens of baby sundews.

They grew and grew, until they were almost big enough to start catching things.

Then one day I watered them with the wrong kind of water—and every single one died.

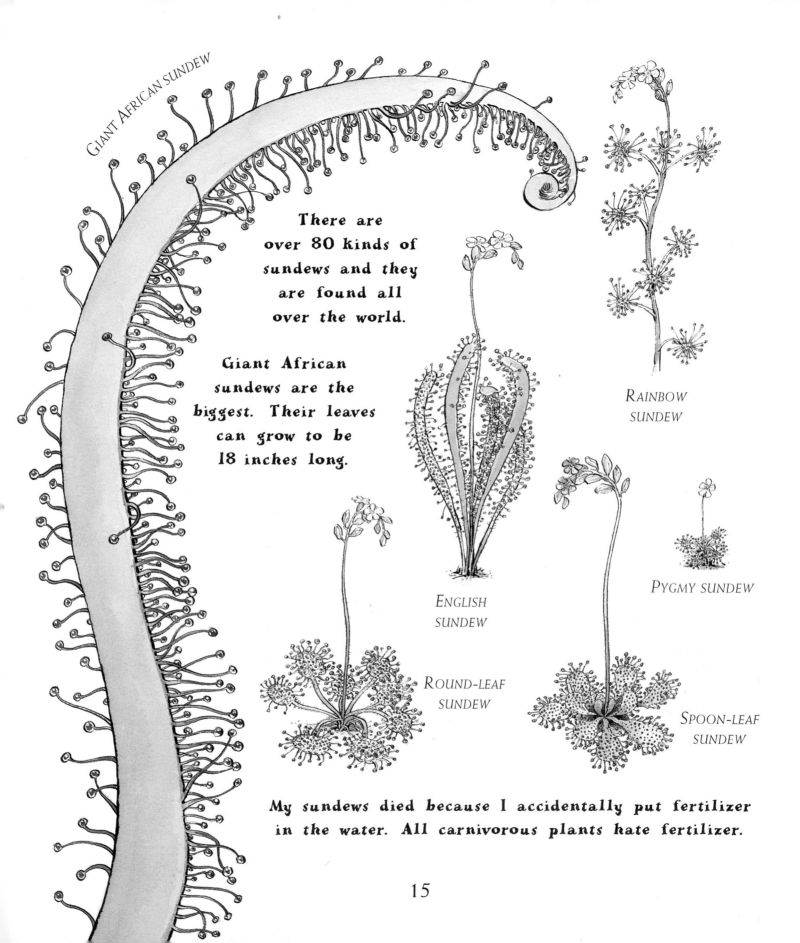

GIANT AFRICAN SUNDEW

There are
over 80 kinds of
sundews and they
are found all
over the world.

Giant African
sundews are the
biggest. Their leaves
can grow to be
18 inches long.

RAINBOW
SUNDEW

ENGLISH
SUNDEW

PYGMY SUNDEW

ROUND-LEAF
SUNDEW

SPOON-LEAF
SUNDEW

My sundews died because I accidentally put fertilizer
in the water. All carnivorous plants hate fertilizer.

I gave up on sundews after that,

but I did grow a Venus flytrap. It lived

on the windowsill and caught insects.

Each of its leaves had a hinge down

the center, several little trigger hairs,

and a spiky rim.

When a fly or a wasp walked

over a leaf, it was perfectly safe

if it didn't touch any of the hairs.

It was even safe if it touched just

one of the hairs. But if it touched

two of the hairs, then...

Venus flytraps grow in only one small part of the southeastern United States. They are rare now because people have drained many of the marshes where they once lived.

Small insects such as ants can
escape from a Venus flytrap—
they're not big enough
to be worth eating.

But flies and wasps
are a different story.
Once caught, the more
they struggle the tighter
the leaf presses together.

When the leaf is
fully closed, it
begins to dissolve
its victim.

19

My Venus flytrap seemed
quite happy, so I thought I'd try
growing something even bigger.
The next plant I got was a
cobra lily.

Cobra lilies get
their name because
their leaves look like
cobras, not because
they eat them!

20

This one caught insects, too, but it didn't actually do very much. It had leaves like funnels, with a slippery rim and a little pool at the bottom.

When insects crawled inside, they fell into the pool and couldn't climb out. So they stayed there and became bug soup for the lily.

Cobra lilies grow along the western coast of the United States. Their leaves can be up to 18 inches long.

21

I was very happy with my cobra lily. Surely it was the biggest carnivorous plant of all. But then my friend told me about pitcher plants.

Pitchers are even bigger, she said, but they are very difficult to grow. In that case, I thought, I'll just go and find some wild ones.

Pitcher plants are found in tropical countries. Like most other carnivorous plants, they usually grow where there is hardly any soil or where the soil is very poor.

So I went—

all the way to Malaysia.

And there, growing up the trees at the edge of the jungle, were hundreds of pitcher plants. Fat red ones, thin yellow ones, curly green ones, all waiting for flies.

The pitchers'
leaves look like
vases, and they
catch insects in
the same way that
cobra lilies do.

There are some kinds
of spiders, and even some
small tree frogs, that
are able to live inside
the pitchers. They
cling to the slippery
sides and grab the
insects that fall in.

25

I didn't see the biggest
pitcher plant of all, though.
It's called the Rajah pitcher plant
and it grows on the tallest
mountain in Borneo.

It has pitchers the size of
footballs. People say it can even
catch some kinds of squirrels,
but I'm not convinced.

The mountain is called Kinabalu.
It is over 13,000 feet high.
The Rajah pitcher plant only
grows there and it's even rarer
than the Venus flytrap.

One day I'll go and see for myself...

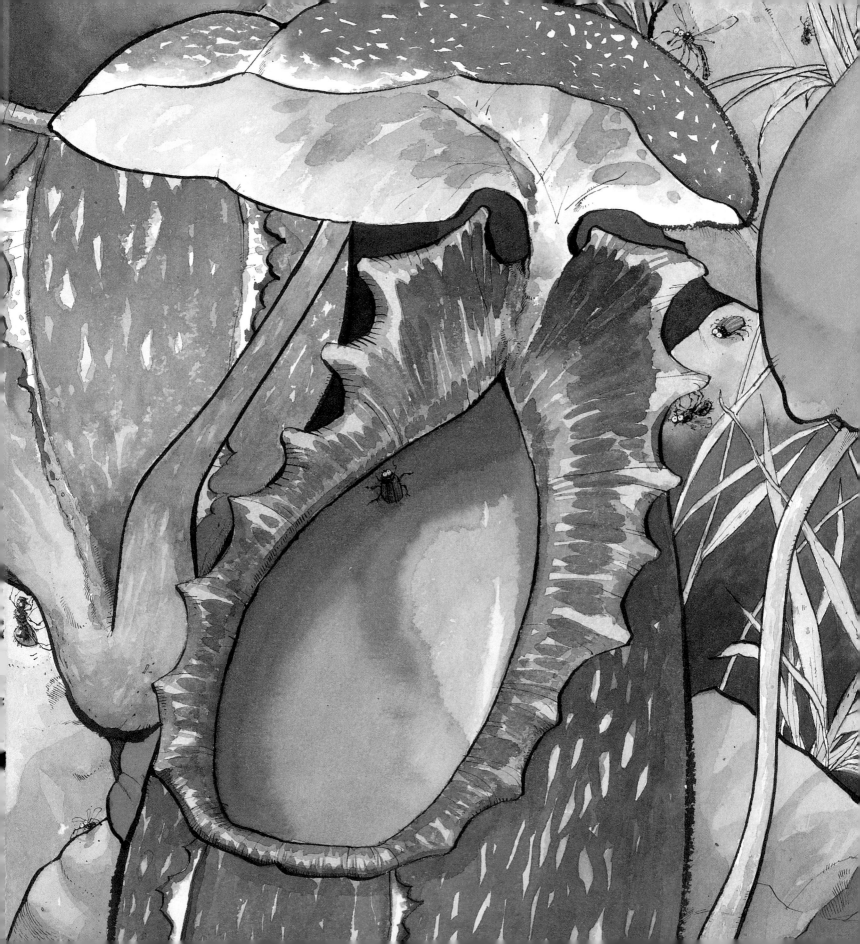

INDEX

Look up the pages to find out about all these
carnivorous plant things. Don't forget to
look at both kinds of words: this kind
and **this kind**.